Tropical Rain Forest: A Political Ecology of Hegemonic Myth Making

Philip Stott

Published by the IEA Environment Unit, 1999

First published in November 1999 by
The Environment Unit
The Institute of Economic Affairs
2 Lord North Street
Westminster
London SW1P 3LB

IEA Studies on the Environment No. 15
All rights reserved
ISBN 0-255 36485-7

Many IEA publications are translated into languages other than
English or are reprinted. Permission to translate or to reprint should
be sought from the General Director at the address above.

Printed in Great Britain by
Hartington Fine Arts Limited, Lancing, West Sussex
Set in Times New Roman and Univers

Contents

Foreword

Our attachment to the *tropical rain forest* has grown over the past hundred years from a minority colonial pursuit to mainstream environmental obsession. The *tropical rain forest* has variously been assumed to be the world's most important repository of biological diversity and 'the lungs of the planet'. As Philip Stott shows in this magnificent monograph, neither claim has any basis in fact.

The Northern environmentalist conception of the *tropical rain forest* is far removed from the ecological realities of the places it purports to denote. Most of the 'million year old forest' to which environmentalists sentimentally refer turns out to have existed for less than 20,000 years. During the last ice age the tropics were colder and drier than today and probably more closely resembled the savanna grasslands of East Africa. Most of the abundant plants and insects of the so-called *tropical rain forest* are equally novel, having co-evolved with the trees.

Claims regarding the fragility of the ecosystems in tropical areas are similarly awry. Recent research suggests that a clear-cut area will return to forest with a similar level of biological diversity to the original within twenty years. Moreover, cutting the forest at the edges tends to increase, not decrease, biological diversity, because it creates diversity of habitat (de Miranda 1994). Ironically, the mythical 'climax rain forest' would be a barren place: no new species would evolve because there would be no new environmental niches to be filled.

The myth of the *tropical rain forest* suits the purposes of Northern environmentalists, who are essentially ultra-conservative: for them all change is bad. Witness their paranoid obsession with the climate, which seeks to achieve the impossibility of climate stability regardless of cost (when the climate appeared to be cooling in the 1970s, their objective was to keep the planet warm; now that it appears to be warming, they want to keep us cool). By claiming that the tropical rain forest is both static and fragile, environmentalists justify demands for restrictions on the conversion of 'virgin forest' to other uses.

Yet the history of the world has been one of evolutionary change. If we attempt to maintain stasis, we risk limiting our

4

ability to adapt to change when it inevitably comes. The ultra-conservative strategy encouraged by environmentalists is far more dangerous to human survival than a strategy that embraces risk and change.

Calls for the *tropical rain forest* to be preserved are founded on the implied presumption that the people living in tropical regions are merely there to protect a western construct. This denigrates their rights and dehumanises them. Just as the colonial administrators sought to reduce the numbers of livestock kept by Africans, claiming that the tribes-people did not know how to manage their land (Morris, 1995), environmentalists demand that indigenous people be discouraged from converting land to agricultural purposes or to plantation forest. This is, at base, little more then a new form of colonialism.

The appropriate use of a particular area of land is most likely to be discovered by people with strong tenurial rights in that land, since such rights create incentives to invest time and money discovering which of the alternative uses is best. Where people cannot own land, or where the costs of protecting land are very high, they have little incentive to invest in conservation. By contrast, where land may be owned and costs of protecting it are relatively low, individuals have incentives to invest in conservation because they know that they will be able to reap the rewards of those investments.

If people in developing countries are to escape from the mire of poverty in which so many continue to live, it is essential that they have secure rights of tenure and are free to do with their land what they will. Some may make mistakes, some may fail in their attempts to manage the land, but many will be successful and those successes will be emulated. Through a process of experimentation – trial, error and emulation – people will come to learn how best to manage the land. The environment will then be managed in ways that are best for humanity as a whole, not according to the whims of a minority of eco-imperialists. Giving rights to people, not to the environment, is not only best for the people, but is also best for the environment.

Philip Stott provides an eloquent deconstruction of the ideas that have led to the mythical western idea of the *tropical rain forest*, which constrains our ability to understand the environments of developing countries and has enabled the eco-imperialist vision to flourish. As with all Environment Unit publications, the views expressed are those of the author and not of the Institute (which has no corporate view), its Directors, Advisors, or Trustees.

October 1999   *JULIAN MORRIS*
                                    Co-Director, Environment Unit

References

de Miranda, E. E. (1994) 'Tropical Rain Forests – Myths and Realities' in *Environmental Gore: A constructive response to 'Earth in the Balance'*. Ed. John A. Baden; San Francisco, USA.

Morris, J. (1995) 'Political Economy of Land Degradation, London: IEA.

The Author

Philip Stott is Professor of Biogeography in the University of London, where he teaches in the Department of Geography at the School of Oriental and African Studies. He was Head of Department for some seven years. Professor Stott has researched on the ecology of the tropics for over twenty-five years and he is an authority on tropical rain forests, savannas, and South East Asia. He is currently Editor of the internationally important *Journal of Biogeography* published by Blackwell Science at Oxford, and he has just written a textbook, *Global Environmental Change*, with Dr Peter Moore and Professor Bill Challoner. Professor Stott also broadcasts widely and he was recently featured on BBC Radio 4's 'Frontiers'. He maintains a critical Web Site on tropical ecology, 'The Anti-Ecohype Web Site' at http://www.ecotrop.org that has many links and educational resources. He is married to Dr Anne Stott, a historian, has two children, Katherine and Emilie, and is passionate about master prints, drawings and Early Music.

Constructing the 'Tropical Rain Forest'

'When *I* use a word,' Humpty Dumpty said in a rather scornful tone. 'it means just what I choose it to mean. – neither more nor less'.

'The question is,' said Humpty Dumpty. 'which is to be master – that's all'.

Lewis Carroll:
'Through the Looking-Glass, and what Alice found there'
Chapter VI: Humpty Dumpty (1872).[1]

'Tropical rain forest' does not exist as an object; it is a human construct and is thus subject to myth making on a grand scale. According to the 'Worry Index' issued at the end of 1998 by the Infratest Institute. the biggest anxiety in Germany is the perceived destruction of tropical rain forest, a fear shared by 86 per cent of the German population.[2] The aims of this booklet are to deconstruct such Northern[3] 'Green' neo-colonial concerns about the entity 'tropical rain forest' and to analyse critically the myths employed to add legitimacy to such concerns. It is argued that these myths have become examples of what are termed 'hegemonic myths'. which exclude other myths from world policy debate.

---

[1]   Charles Lutwidge Dodgson ('Lewis Carroll') (1832–98). *Through the Looking-Glass, and what Alice found there*. London: Macmillan (1872).

[2]   See: 'Germans turning Green with anxiety'. *The Times*. Tuesday. December 29. p. 10 (1998).

[3]   The term 'Northern' is here used to refer to the rich countries of 'the North', especially North America and Europe, in contradistinction to the less-developed countries (LDCs) comprising 'the South'. The terms are not, however, strictly geographical in character, with countries such as Japan and Australia forming part of 'the North' for certain analytical purposes. *Cf.* Footnote 8.

The linguistic entity

Energy and (bio)mass[4] are essentially continuous over the surface of the Earth. Any division, or interruption, of this continuity is largely arbitrary and is based on a narrow range of selected criteria. If the entity of division is given a name (or signifier[5]), like 'tropical rain forest', it becomes a linguistic unit fully comprehended only by those who share an understanding of the specific criteria employed. These criteria may be culturally determined. Different criteria, or a different application of the same criteria, will result in a different linguistic category. Certain connections between a signifier (the material notation, such as: **t.r.e.e**) and the signified (the mental concept stimulated by the signifier, such as '**treeness**') are so close that they are grasped comprehensively at an early age by all within the same linguistic group. Even under these circumstances, however, there still remains a degree of arbitrariness in the link with the thing, or object, in the real world. Whereas 'cup' and 'cupness' clearly relate to an object in which the boundaries are not noticeably fluid, when exactly, by contrast, is a savanna(h)[6] woody species a tree and not a shrub?[7]

In some linguistic entities, including 'tropical rain forest' and 'savanna', the boundaries of the 'object' may be so intrinsically fluid that such entities have to be socially constructed, formally taught and learned, while no real thing, or

---

[4] 'Biomass' is the total weight of organic matter covering the surface of the Earth. It is measured, usually by dry weight, for a unit area at a given point in time, e.g. 600 t ha^{-1}.

[5] A 'signifier' is the sound image made by a word, such as 'lion'. The *concept* of a lion is known as the 'signified'. This distinction (or 'dyad') was emphasised by the Swiss linguistic philosopher, Ferdinand de Saussure (1857–1913), in *Cours de linguistique générale*, first published in 1916 from extant notes taken by his students. See: *Course in General Linguistics*. London: Fontana/Collins (1974); also: Madan Sarup, *An Introductory Guide to Post-structuralism and Postmodernism*. Hemel Hempstead, Herts: Harvester Wheatsheaf, 2nd edn (1993).

[6] Savannas – or 'savannahs' in the pre-1956 spelling – are a perceived vegetation type of the lowlands of the seasonal tropics and sub-tropics. The name is derived from a 16th Century Spanish word *zavanna* (modern Spanish: *sabana*), and it was first recorded in 1535 by Oviedo as coming originally from Carib, a language found in the southern West Indies. Savanna vegetation comprises a mixture of grasses and herbs with woody elements, ranging from dwarf shrubs to large umbrella-shaped trees.

[7] Because of this problem, many ecologists resort to referring, somewhat inelegantly, to 'the woody element' in savanna vegetation.

object, exists at all (Figure 1). Therefore, whoever has the mastery, to use Humpty Dumpty's word, over the content of such constructed names also holds power over the use of those names. It is our purpose to explore these power relations, which constitute the heart of any analytical political ecology.[8] Who currently wields power over the content of the linguistic unit 'tropical rain forest'? What are the origins of this content? How is this power employed, and for what political purposes? What is the 'science' behind the content of the name? And what is the morality behind the 'science' and the content?

'Tropical rain forest'

With regard to 'tropical rain forest', it must be recognized from the start that there has been little agreement over either the criteria of selection or the linguistic entity itself. There have been many 'tropical rain forests', and the linguistic and mythic content of the name has varied greatly in time and space. Throughout its linguistic history, the dominant content has thus changed markedly and, with it, both the linguistic and perceived boundaries of the entity designated as 'tropical rain forest'. For most Northerners, tropical rain forest remains little more than a media construct, or a film set, a riotous 'jungle' (see p. 17) of climbers and creepers, with Tarzan swinging from tree to tree.

Credit for the creation of the linguistic entity 'tropical rain forest' is normally accorded to a German scholar, Andreas Franz Wilhelm Schimper (1856–1901) (Figure 2), who first used the term *tropische Regenwald* in his founding work on ecology, *Planzengeographie auf physiologischer Grundlage*, published in 1898. This was translated into English in 1903 as *Plant-geography upon a physiological basis*.[9] Schimper was deeply

---

8 "…changes will not occur without considerable struggle since they necessitate the transformation of a series of highly unequal power relationships upon which the present system is based: First Third Worlds, rich/poor or rulers/ruled." Raymond L. Bryant & Sinéad Bailey. *Third World Political Ecology*. London & New York: Routledge, p.3 (1997).

9 Andreas Franz Wilhelm Schimper, *Pflanzengeographie auf physiologischer Grundlage*. Jena: Gustav-Fischer (1898); English translation by W.R. Fisher, P. Groom and I.B. Balfour. *Plant-geography upon a physiological basis*. Oxford: Oxford University Press (1903). See: T.C. Whitmore, *Tropical rain forests of the Far East*. Oxford: Clarendon Press. 2nd edn (1984).

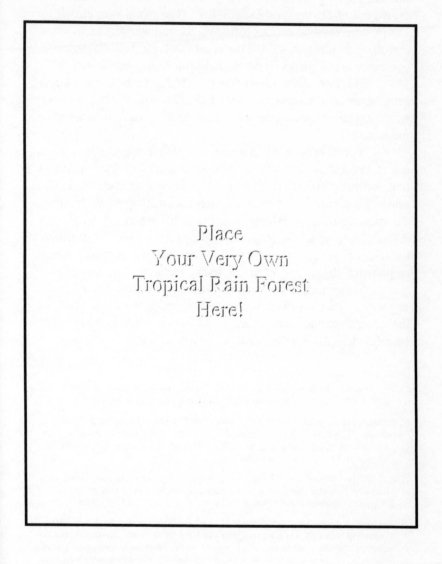

Figure 1.   Impose your own 'tropical rain forest' construction on to the white square.

imbued with the ethos of the late-nineteenth Century, which had grown out of Darwin and Darwinism[10]. The world was viewed as comprising 'organic entities' attached to, and adapted to, the land and the prevailing climate. This is particularly well illustrated in two other major works of the period, *Anthropogeographie* (1882, 1891) and *Politische Geographie* (1897), both by a human geographer and natural scientist, Friedrich Ratzel (1844–1904), who even talked of the political 'state' as an organism attached to the land.[11]

For Schimper, by contrast, the organismic elements were not states, but groups of plants (and to a lesser extent animals) that formed units of 'vegetation'. His book thus focuses on the selection of criteria for the definition and naming of these units, the most famous of which is perhaps his entity 'tropical rain forest'. In doing so, Schimper firmly established what is normally thought of as the synecological[12] approach to ecology, which emphasises the synthesis of all living elements into identifiable *named* functioning units, such as plant associations, communities or biomes. This approach was eventually to give rise, in 1935, to the concept of the 'ecosystem'[13] and, much later, to other more fanciful ideas, such as James E. Lovelock's 'Gaia'.[14]

---

[10] See: Eugene Cittadino. *Nature as the Laboratory. Darwinian plant ecology in the German Empire, 1880–1900.* Cambridge: Cambridge University Press (1990).

[11] Friedrich Ratzel. *Anthropogeographie, oder Grundzüge der Anwendung der Erdkunde auf die Geschichte.* Stuttgart: Engelhorn (1882); *Anthropogeographie II: Die geographische Verbrietung des Menschen.* Stuttgart: Engelhorn (1891); *Politische Geographie.* Munich: Oldenburg (1897).

[12] As will be stressed later, 'synecology' must be compared and contrasted with 'autecology', in which the focus is on the individual organism, or species, and not on the grouping of organisms into synthetic language units.

[13] The term 'ecosystem' was introduced in 1935 by a British ecologist, Sir Arthur George Tansley (1871–1955), and is a *concept* in which the living (biotic) community and the non-living (abiotic) environment are viewed as a functioning integrated system. Ecosystems no more exist than do tropical rain forests, but until recently they have remained the main approach to study in modern synecology.

[14] See: James E. Lovelock. *Gaia, a new look at life on Earth.* Oxford & New York: Oxford University Press (1979); James E. Lovelock. *The ages of Gaia: a biography of our living Earth.* New York: Norton (1988); Lawrence E. Joseph. *Gaia: the growth of an idea.* New York: St. Martin's Press (1990); Stephen H. Schneider & Penelope J. Boston (eds.). *Scientists on Gaia.* Cambridge, Mass: MIT (1991); Edward Goldsmith. *The way: an ecological world-view.* Athens, GA: University of Georgia Press (1998).

For Schimper, the dryland tropics comprise four linguistic entities in which trees are seen as the characteristic dominants, or co-dominants, of the vegetation: these are tropical rain forest, monsoon forest, savanna forest, and thorn forest. Tropical rain forest is indicated as the linguistic unit typifying the ever-wet tropics, in contrast to the seasonal tropics, which are occupied by the leaf-shedding monsoon, savanna and thorn forests. Schimper's descriptive content of the term was as follows: 'evergreen, hygrophilous[15] in character, at least thirty metres high, rich in thick stemmed lianes, and

in woody as well as herbaceous epiphytes.'[16] This diagnosis represents the first 'scientific' definition of the term, and, although it has been largely ignored, altered or played about with by many later ecologists, often leading to total confusion, it is still considered 'helpful' by some scholars.

And 'helpful' is the appropriate word. The Algerian-born French philosopher Jacques Derrida's (b.1930)[17] concept of 'sous rature', or 'under erasure', unquestionably interprets the term as used by most scientists. Many ecologists accept that 'tropical rain forest' embraces a flawed concept, but one that is still vital to begin to make some sense of the complexity of the tropical world. The entity might thus be better presented, following both Martin Heidegger (1889–1976)[18] and Derrida, 'sous rature', that is, first printed and then crossed out. We should write: 'tropical rain forest ~~tropical rain forest~~', indicating at one and the same time that the term is *inadequate yet necessary*. It will be argued later, however, that even this degree of linguistic caution is no longer acceptable, because the concept of 'tropical rain forest' is now so radically flawed and abused through the development of Northern

---

[15] 'Hygrophilous' means 'water-loving'.

[16] Schimper (1903), p.260. Lianes, or lianas, are woody climbing plants; epiphytes are plants that live on the surface of other plants without, by contrast to parasites, significantly damaging their host.

[17] The leading figure in contemporary deconstruction. See: Jacques Derrida, *Writing and Difference*. London: Routledge & Kegan Paul (1978); also Chapter 2, 'Derrida and deconstruction' in Madan Sarup, *An Introductory Guide to Post-structuralism and Postmodernism*. Hemel Hempstead, Herts: Harvester Wheatsheaf, 2nd edn (1993).

[18] The philosopher, Martin Heidegger, frequently crossed out the word 'Being', i.e. ~~Being~~, believing it to transcend any signification.

Figure 2. Andreas Franz Schimper (1856-1901), who first invented the linguistic entity *tropische Regenwald* ('tropical rain forest') in 1898.

hegemonic myths that it is has become too inadequate and too politically dangerous.

Myth making before Schimper

Before Schimper and the late-19th Century, it is important to note that few people had any concept of 'tropical rain forest' as such, or a consistent signifier for it[19], with the possible exception of the

---

[19] Prior to 1898, it might well be argued that the semiotic position was 'integrationist' in the sense espoused by Roy Harris in *Signs, language and communication*. London & New York: Routledge (1998). This means that signs presuppose communication, with signs as products of observation. In 1898, and after, with regard to 'tropical rain forest', the position becomes, by contrast, 'segregationist', in which communication pre-supposes signs and signs are pre-requisites of communication. Such potential shifts in ontological primacy merit much further research.

German polymath, Alexander von Humboldt (1769–1859)[20], whose organismic approach to NatureNature foreshadowed the post-Darwinian era. Little had changed from the earliest exuberant European accounts of tropical forest vegetation, well-exemplified in the famous letter of Christopher Columbus (1451–1506) describing his First Voyage of 1492–1493: –

'From this place I saw another island to the east distant from this Juana 54 miles. which I called forthwith Hispana [Hispaniola]; and I sailed to it; and I steered along the northern coast, as at Juana, towards the east. 564 miles.

And the said Juana and the other islands there appear very fertile. This island is surrounded by many very safe and wide harbours. not excelled by any others that I have ever seen. Many great and salubrious rivers flow through it. There are also many very high mountains there. All these islands are very beautiful, and distinguished by various qualities; they are accessible, and full of a great variety of trees stretching up to the stars; the leaves of which I believe are never shed. for I saw them as green and flourishing as they are usually in Spain in the month of May; some of them were blossoming. some were bearing fruit, some were in other conditions; each one was thriving in its own way. The nightingale and various other birds without number were singing, in the month of November. when I was exploring them.

There are besides in the said island Juana seven or eight kinds of palm trees. which far excel ours in height and beauty, just as all the other trees. herbs. and fruits do.'[21]

---

[20] Alexander von Humboldt. *Kosmos: Entwurf einer physischen Weltbeschreibung.* 5 vols. Stuttgart: Cotta (1845–62); see also: Richard Hartshorne. 'The Nature of Geography. A critical survey of current thought in the light of the past.' Lancaster, Pennsylvania: *Annals of the Association of American Geographers* **29**, pp. 173–658 (1939).

[21] Translated from: *In laudem Serenissimi Ferdinandi Hispaniaerum regis, Bethicae et regni Granatæ. obsidio, victoria, et triüphus, Et de Insulis in mari Indico nuper inuentis.* Basel: Johann Bergmann de Olpe ('I.B') (1494). This is the 1494 Basle Edition of the Latin version of the Columbus Letter, which was originally dated 15 February 1493 and first published in Spanish at Barcelona: Pedro Posa (April 1493). See the following Web Sites for full details and translations:– (a) http://cedar. evansville.edu/~wc102web/102co.html: (b) http://www.usm.maine.edu/~maps/columbus/.

In this oft-quoted passage, Columbus was participating in the creation of a European tradition, or set of 'myths', with regard to tropical vegetation that would persist to the present-day neo-colonial 'Green' interpretation of Schimper's 'tropical rain forest', but one which especially flourished during Europe's direct colonial domination of tropical lands. The tradition involves, first, an orientalist[22] view of the plants as 'exotic'; secondly, an analogy with the home country ('as they are usually in Spain in the month of May'); and finally, an image of incredible fertility, fecundity and diversity. The same tradition also flourished in the Asian tropics, especially with regard to the forests of South East Asia. Here, for example, is Guy Madoc's[23] romantic early-20th Century account of colonial Malaya beyond the world of Kuala Lumpur: –

'When we got beyond the rubber estates and saw the wilderness of the jungle, that, I think, is really what got me – that first impression of the jungle as a mysterious and almost impenetrable place.

Hundreds of miles of jungle over rolling mountains, exciting torrents coming down through the jungle, and when the torrents levelled out into smooth river, green padi-fields and little Malay kampongs, dotted around in the shade of fruit trees and coconut trees. It was all I had imagined of rural Malaya.'[24]

Thus, by the 19th and early-20th Centuries, this process of myth making had hardly broken out of the 16th Century mould. It is true that tropical 'forest' as an entity was now recognized as against 'savanna(h)', but without any precision or clear content as to a 'type'. This is well shown by Madoc's use of the word 'jungle', which entered Anglo-Indian parlance during the mid-18th

---

[22] Refers to 'Orientalism', a complex discourse on power, domination and hegemony developed by Edward Said concerning the relationships between the West (Occident) and the Rest (Orient). See: E.W. Said, *Orientalism*. New York: Vintage (1979) and *Culture and Imperialism*. London: Chatto & Windus (1993).

[23] Guy Madoc joined the Federated Malay States (FMS) Police in 1930, and was interned in Singapore in 1942. He was in CID Headquarters, London, from 1950, forming the Special Branch in 1952. He retired from Government service in 1959.

[24] In: Charles Allen (ed.), *Tales from the South China Seas. Images of the British in South-East Asia in the Twentieth Century*. London: Futura (1984), p. 113.

Century from the Hindi and Marathi *jangal* (from the Sanskrit for 'dry', 'dryland', 'desert'), meaning 'desert', 'waste', or 'forest' in the Norman French sense of 'uncultivated or unenclosed land'.[25] Like the word 'forest', 'jungle' also appears to have transferred its meaning in Anglo-Indian from 'unenclosed waste' to 'land covered with wild wood'. One of the very earliest references to 'jungle' appears in the 'Journals' of Major James Rennell, the first Surveyor-General of India, written for the information of the Governors of Bengal during his surveys of the Ganges and Brahmaputra Rivers in 1764–1767: 'We find the depths of Water from 34 to 8 Cubits (in ye dry Season), the Banks being mostly covered with Jungle we have very troublesome work to survey them.'[26] On approaching the Sunderbans, Rennell seems to distinguish 'jungly' from 'woody', and later he observes that there are many 'Tygers' in the 'Jungle'.

Jungle was definitely not, therefore, a true precursor of Schimper's 'tropical rain forest' in any meaningful sense, the earliest connotations always being tropical land with underwood, long grass, and a tumble of vegetation. Its use as a popular, if somewhat misleading, simile for 'tropical rain forest' is a much later 20th Century phenomenon. The commonest descriptors remained simplistic and very general, including 'jungle', 'great forest', 'black forest', 'gloomy forest' and, in South America, 'Atlantic forest' or '*selva*', a word derived from Spanish and Portuguese, but ultimately from the Latin, *silva* ('forest').

Thus, writing nearly 400 years later, the engineer and naturalist, Thomas Belt (1832–1878), although presenting us with an obvious link to Schimper, continues to employ a mythic language little removed from that of Columbus: –

---

[25] See for a full discussion of the word 'jungle': Francis Zimmermann, *The jungle and the aroma of meats. An ecological theme in Hindu medicine.* Berkeley: University of California Press (1987). See also Henry Yule and A. C. Burnell, *Hobson-Jobson. A glossary of colloquial Anglo-Indian words and phrases, and of kindred terms, etymological, historical, geographical and discursive.* London: John Murray.

[26] July 10, 1764. See: T.H.D. La Touche, *The Journals of Major James Rennell, first Surveyor General of India, written for the information of the Governors of Bengal during his surveys of the Ganges and Brahmaputra Rivers 1764–1767.* Calcutta: The Asiatic Society. p. 20 (1910).

...we entered the great forest, the black margin of which we had seen for many miles, that extends from this point to the Atlantic...

...we entered the primeval forest.

...great trees towered up, carrying their crowns out of sight amongst a canopy of foliage; lianas wound round every trunk and hung from every bough, passing from tree to tree, and entangling the giants in a great net-work of coiling cables, as the serpents did Laocoon...

...the Atlantic forest, bathed in the rains distilled from the north-east trades, is ever verdant...Unknown are the autumn tints, the bright browns and yellows of English woods...A ceaseless round of ever-active life weaves the forest scenery of the tropics into one monotonous whole, of which the component parts exhibit in detail untold variety and beauty.'[27]

Here indeed is a sense of 'forest', but it is just as exotic, non-European, and teeming with 'variety and beauty' as that of Columbus; and to this is now added a potent new European 'myth,' the idea that the 'dark forest' is 'primeval', a refuge surviving from a classical Golden Age of the World, unsullied by human sin. Moreover, the forest is conceived as 'one monotonous whole', a woven organismic entity, an image that would come to haunt the 20th Century view of Schimper's 1898 construction.

Tropical Rain Forest as an 'Organism'

The late-19th Century construction of tropical rain forest, and other vegetation units, as organismic entities in their own right was soon to lead in the early-20th Century to the development of a theory, called successional theory, to account for the evolution, growth and ontology of such 'organisms'. This theory was synthesised in the significant contributions of two ecologists, an American, Frederick E. Clements (1870–1945), and, in Britain, Sir Arthur George Tansley (1871–1955), who jointly espoused the

---

[27] Quotations selected from Thomas Belt, *The Naturalist in Nicaragua*. London: Edward Bumpus. 2nd Edn (1888) (first published in 1874); described by Charles Darwin in 1874 as "...the best of all natural history journals which have ever been published." See: Francis Darwin (ed.). *The Life and Letters of Charles Darwin, including an Autobiographical Chapter*. 3 vols. London: John Murray, Vol. III, p.188.

concept of the 'climax formation'.[28] This concept would come to dominate, until the 1960s, the thinking of scientific ecologists, but also, more worryingly, late-20th Century 'Green' ideas.

In 1916, Clements defined the climax formation as 'the adult organism, of which all initial and medial stages are but stages of development.'[29] Vegetation, whether initiated on a bare soil surface or over water, was seen as following a natural succession towards an adult stage, the 'climax', which would be in balance, or equilibrium, with the prevailing ecological determinant. It should be noted that this is an entirely Darwinian approach which treats 'vegetation', like 'tropical rain forest', as an individual organism, say a teak tree or a tiger, that evolves, grows and adapts to its surroundings. It was a theory of its time and place, and, as we shall see later, one challenged even at the very outset of its formulation (*cf.* footnote 48).

For Clements, there was really only one key ecological determinant of vegetation succession, namely climate, with one final adult phase, which was termed the 'climatic climax'. His interpretation is thus often characterised as the 'monoclimax' approach.[30] By contrast, Tansley argued that, in addition to climate, there was a range of other ecological determinants, including geology/soils (the edaphic climax[31]) and even humans (the anthropogenic climax). Tansley is therefore thought of as adopting a 'polyclimax' approach. Both, however, regarded tropical rain forest as the climatic climax, the natural adult organism, of the humid tropics.

---

[28] See especially: F.E. Clements, *Plant succession: an analysis of the development of vegetation*. Washington, D.C.: Carnegie Inst. Washington, Publication No. **242** (1916); F.E. Clements, 'Nature and structure of the climax'. *Journal of Ecology* **24**, pp. 252–284 (1936); A.G. Tansley, 'The classification of vegetation'. *Journal of Ecology* **8**, pp. 118–149 (1920); and the classic book A.G. Tansley, *The British Islands and their vegetation*. Cambridge: Cambridge University Press (1939). See also: J.W. Weaver & F.E. Clements, *Plant ecology*. New York and London: McGraw-Hill, 2nd edn (1938).

[29] F.E. Clements, *Plant succession: an analysis of the development of vegetation*. Washington, D.C.: Carnegie Inst. Washington, Publication No. **242** (1916).

[30] See: Philip Stott, 'The History of Biogeography', pp. 1–24 in J. A. Taylor (ed.) *Themes in Biogeography*. London: Croom Helm (1984).

[31] 'Edaphic' (from the Greek *edaphos*, 'bottom' or 'soil') refers to those physical and chemical characteristics of soil which especially influence vegetation and animals.

Following the later development of the ecosystem concept by Tansley in 1935[32], such climatic climaxes were seen as exhibiting a particularly striking system characteristic, namely homeostasis, or the inherent ability to self-regulate themselves in the face of small variations in the flux of energy and/or mass through the system. Climatic climaxes were therefore regarded as essentially 'stable' communities, largely in balance with their prevailing environment. In the light of all we now know of climate change, this viewpoint seems frankly bizarre, but, in 1936, Clements[33] could still assert unthinkingly '...that stabilisation is the universal tendency of all vegetation under the ruling climate, and that climaxes are characterised by a high degree of stability when reckoned in thousands or even millions of years.'

Yet, Clements and Tansley were clearly speaking to a world that wanted to hear such a message of stability and harmony. It met a deep human need. The European myth of the primeval forest, once romantically promulgated by naturalists such as Thomas Belt and poets like Henry Wadsworth Longfellow (1807–1882)[34], was at last bolstered by a powerful 'scientific' theory, so that the tropical rain forest could be constructed into that great undisturbed 60 million-year old 'cathedral' of the wild, in balance and harmony with Nature, which is so beloved of Northern conservationists today.[35]

And to disturb such harmony, such equilibrium, soon became regarded as a sin against Nature. Clements went on to affirm that:

> Man alone can destroy the stability of the climax during the long period of control by its climate, and he accomplishes this by fragments in consequence of destruction that is selective, partial or complete and continually renewed.

---

[32] A.G. Tansley, 'The use and abuse of vegetational concepts and terms.' *Ecology* **16**, pp. 284–307 (1935).

[33] F.E. Clements, 'Nature and structure of the climax'. *Journal of Ecology* **24**, pp. 252–284 (1936).

[34] "This is the forest primeval", Henry Wadsworth Longfellow, in *Evangeline* (1847).

[35] For example, the opening paragraph of Chris C. Park's *Tropical rainforests*. London & New York: Routledge (1992): "Rainforests (better known to many people as jungles) have been the dominant form of vegetation in the tropics for literally millions of years,..." (p. 1).

The process of the criminalisation of human actions with regard to the environment had begun, and the construction of the current 'Green' paradigm of the tropical rain forest was underway. In the United Kingdom, this complete post-Schimperian myth was then firmly consolidated by the publication in 1952 of Paul Richards' *The tropical rain forest: an ecological study*, which has remained a widely-used textbook until the present day.[36] A very belated second edition appeared in 1996.

---

[36] P. W. Richards, *The tropical rain forest: an ecological study*. Cambridge: Cambridge University Press (1952). See also: P. W. Richards, *The tropical rain forest*. Cambridge: Cambridge University Press, 2nd Edn (1996).

Deconstructing the Mythical Content

Tropical forests are both the fearsome Jungle of our fantasy and the fertile Eden of our myth.

From the 'Rainforest Information Page' of the
Rainforest Alliance Web Site (New York)
(URL: http://www.rainforest-alliance.org/)
Accessed at 16.00 on 22nd July 1998.

This brief analytical history of the construction of the entity 'tropical rain forest' can now be used to begin to deconstruct contemporary tropical rain forest texts, especially those relating to the 'Green' paradigm, or dominant system of scientific thought. In doing so, it is important to recognise the primacy of language in directing our thinking under such paradigms.

Language controls

According to the Freudian psychoanalyst, Jacques Lacan (1901–1981)[37], the way we think at any one time is governed above all by what he terms the *'points de capiton'* ('upholstery buttons'). These fix the fabric of meaning onto the structure of our signs or language, just like the buttons that attach the leather covering to a chair or settee. *'Points de capiton'* represent the key signifiers, or dominant language, defining the entity in question. Ultimately, they comprise both a mythic language for that entity as well as a metalanguage, the overarching set of language controls which govern everything that is written, spoken, drawn or acted upon with regard to the concept. *'Points de capiton'* thus determine both the content and the meaning of the entity. In many instances, a master, or key, signifier is ultimately 'sealed' into the discourse by a range of related words, as with **'freedom'** in politics. Unfortunately, in the case of tropical rain forest, one influential key signifier is the now much-outdated metaword used by Clements and Tansley, **'equilibrium'**, and this is one major factor

---

[37] Jacques Lacan, *Écrits: a selection*. London: Tavistock (1977); see also Chapter 1, 'Lacan and psychoanalysis' in Madan Sarup, *An Introductory Guide to Post-structuralism and Postmodernism*. Hemel Hempstead, Herts: Harvester Wheatsheaf, 2nd edn (1993).

leading to a morally misleading and potentially dangerous Northern view of the tropical world.

Tropical rain forest *'points de capiton'*

Interestingly, even a cursory analysis of the *'points de capiton'* employed to 'seal' meaning into any 'Green' text on tropical rain forest demonstrates that they are derived directly from the writings of the European explorers, such as Columbus and Belt, and from the organismic scientists, Schimper, Clements, Tansley, and Richards; that is, from the very history of tropical rain forest construction in Europe and North America outlined above. The intrinsic and extrinsic power of the words used as key signifiers should not be underestimated, and, although their origins and construction tend to be little understood by those who employ them, they form a core mythic language with regard to tropical rain forest which is repeated, like a mantra, in text after text, the world over (see Figure 3). On analysing the character of the language found in ten major Web Site documents about tropical rain forest from around the World Wide Web (1998), the author was staggered to find that the texts fell automatically into two standard language categories, with a division at around 66 per cent and 32 per cent respectively in *all* documents (*cf.* p.28) The language controls seem to be in the very air itself!

It is possible to classify the metawords defining the linguistic entity 'tropical rain forest' into four main sets of *'points de capiton'*. The first set relates to the key signifier, **orientalism** (the 'exotic other', as defined by Edward Said[38]), and includes, among others, 'jungle', 'exuberant', 'luxuriant', 'fertile', 'hothouse', 'diverse', 'richest', 'most complex', 'unrivalled', 'idyllic', 'mysterious', 'vast storehouse', 'unique', and 'exotic'. These remain very much the language of the earliest explorers, like Columbus, and they still strongly characterise popular natural history programmes on both radio and television. Secondly, there

---

[38] E.W. Said, *Orientalism*. New York: Vintage (1979) and *Culture and Imperialism*. London: Chatto & Windus (1993).

MYTHIC LANGUAGE

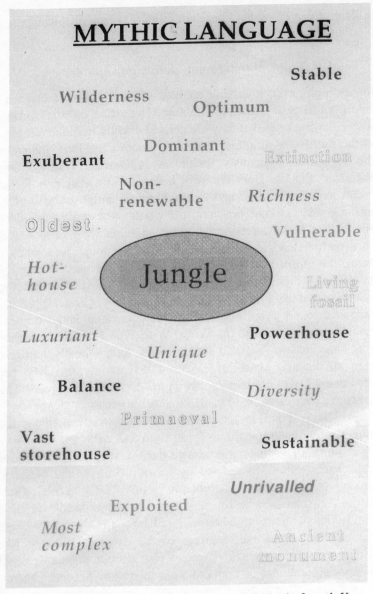

Stable

Wilderness Optimum

Dominant

Exuberant

Extinction

Non-
renewable Richness

Oldest

Vulnerable

Hot-
house **Jungle** Living
fossil

Luxuriant Powerhouse

Unique

Balance Diversity

Primaeval

Vast
storehouse Sustainable

Unrivalled

Exploited

Most
complex Ancient
monument

Figure 3.   Mythic language for the entity: 'tropical rain forest'. Key
signifiers widely employed in 'Green' texts.

are the metawords specifically derived from the organismic **climax** signifiers of Schimper, Clements and Tansley, in particular 'optimum', 'dominant', 'stable', 'balance', 'harmony', 'sustainable', 'equilibrium', and the word 'climax' itself. Thirdly, but clearly related to the latter, are the metawords capturing the **'old age'** signifier of tropical rain forest, such as 'primeval', 'ancient', 'oldest', 'millions of years', 'undisturbed', 'monument', 'the cathedrals of the wild', 'womb of life', and 'living fossil'. Finally, there are the metawords underlining the **vulnerability** signifier, the essential fragility of this rain forest 'Eden' when faced with the sinful actions of humankind, as first stressed by Clements in 1936[39]. This set includes 'exploited', 'damage', 'disturbed', 'problem', 'vulnerable', 'extinction', 'greed', 'destruction', 'unsustainable', 'non-renewable', 'deforestation', 'clearance', and certain more extreme words and phrases, such as 'time-bomb'.

A particularly good example of the use of these metawords to establish the 'tropical rain forest' myth can be found in the opening and closing paragraphs of the 1992 textbook by Chris Park, *Tropical rainforests*[40], which is widely employed in schools and colleges throughout the UK. I have indicated the main metawords by a combination of **bold script** and <u>underlining</u> in the relevant quotations given below: –

'Tropical rainforests are the **most complex** ecosystems on earth. Rainforests (better known to many people as **jungles**) have been the **dominant** form of vegetation in the tropics for **literally millions of years**, and beneath their high canopy lives a **diversity** of species which is **unrivalled** anywhere else on earth.[41]

The **time-bomb** of ecological, environmental, climatic and human **damage** caused by **deforestation** continues to tick, and the **problem** of tropical rainforest **clearance** must remain a priority within international politics.'[42]

---

[39] F.E. Clements, 'Nature and structure of the climax'. *Journal of Ecology* **24**, pp. 252–284 (1936).

[40] Chris C. Park, *Tropical rainforests*. London & New York: Routledge (1992).

[41] Park (1992), p.1.

[42] Park (1992), p.162.

As will be pointed out later, there is not one shred of recent scientific evidence to support the powerful historic and mythic language employed here. Its roots lie entirely in the European and North American construction of the 'tropical rain forest' as a linguistic entity in the late-19th and early-20th Centuries and thus in the writings of the explorers and the Darwinian 'organismic' scientists. This is deeply worrying when one considers that we are quoting from a so-called educational textbook which could well form part of an agreed National School curriculum. It is therefore particularly important to analyse precisely how metawords are embedded in a text, both consciously and unconsciously, to 'load' it in support of a 'Green' construction or paradigm.

Two main techniques are normal. In the first instance, each word is carefully chosen, primarily to set the pure, unsullied, exotic, yet balanced, entity 'tropical rain forest' against human folly, greed, and sin, not to mention chaos and change. It is worth recalling that tropical rain forest is never neutrally affected by human actions, that is, being simply 'used', 'changed', or 'developed'. Deforestation is never 'an opportunity'. By its very nature, tropical rain forest *has to be* 'exploited', 'destroyed', and 'disturbed', while 'deforestation' is always a 'problem' and a 'threat', or, in the hyperbole of Park, a 'time-bomb'. Indeed, so strong is the overall effect of such signifiers that they can alter the meaning of adjacent words, so that a neutral or positive concept, like 'development', automatically becomes, by association, a negative construct.

Secondly, key signifiers are frequently repeated, or spammed, over and over again, either the single word or phrase (e.g. 'dominant'), or different, but cognate, signifiers, one after the other (e.g. richest, diverse, luxuriant, storehouse, complex…), so that their mythical power gradually seeps into the very text. A classic example of this technique occurs on the Greenpeace International Web Site where, under the title 'Ancient Forests', the metaword 'ancient' is repeated no less than twelve times in just a few short paragraphs.[43] It is also worth noting that, in the

---

[43] Greenpeace International: URL: http://greenpeace.org/~forests/ancient.html. Accessed 16.00 on 5th August 1998.

two passages quoted above, key signifiers comprise no less than 12 per cent of the total text of only 78 words.

We can therefore begin to understand the origins and key linguistic controls behind the present-day 'Green' mythical entity, 'tropical rain forest', and perhaps start to grasp exactly why 'tropical rain forest' has become such an environmental shibboleth in late-20th Century Europe, North America, and Australia. However, we must go on to recognise that this historical language has been further developed during the last thirty years or so, often deliberately and knowingly, in order to *guarantee* our unequivocal acceptance of the myth in the modern world. A secondary source of hegemonic myth-making has accordingly been attached to the original historic myths to ensure, first, that we all acknowledge the extreme vulnerability of 'tropical rain forest', and, secondly, that we recognise our deep *'need'* of this entity, 'tropical rain forest', for our very own survival, and for the survival of the whole planet. 'Liking' and 'wanting' are one thing, but they can be debated; *'needing'* is another matter entirely, for it pre-empts further argument.

The language of 'Needing' and 'Vulnerability'

In 1998, the author carried out a detailed study of language use in ten tropical rain forest texts found on the World Wide Web (WWW) employing the QSR NUD*IST 4 Software developed by Qualitative Solutions and Research in Melbourne, Australia.[44] This computer package is designed to aid users in handling non-numerical, unstructured data, such as texts, by supporting processes of coding data in an Index System, searching text or patterns of coding, and ultimately theorizing about the data. The texts employed in this particular instance were all derived from 'Green' organisations with a strong interest in the preservation and conservation of tropical rain forest, ranging from international organisations, such as Greenpeace International, through more local groups (American, Australian, and British), to one

---

[44] QSR stands for Qualitative Solutions and Research Pty Ltd., a Software development company in Melbourne, Australia, and NUD*IST for Non-numerical Unstructured Data Indexing Searching and Theorizing. The company's Web Site is at: http://www.qsr.com.au . See also: Qualitative Solutions and Research Pty Ltd., *QSR NUD*IST 4 User Guide*. QSR Pty Ltd.: La Trobe University, Victoria, 2nd edn (1997).

Fundamentalist Christian Site in Arizona. Some of the Sites were directly involved in the raising of funds to buy up tracts of tropical rain forest. Two further Sites were also accessed, but it was found that their main texts on tropical rain forest were simply copied from, or mirrored, the material already collected at the other Sites. Table 1 gives the full details of the Sites used for this language study.

Figure 4 presents the results of the analysis of the ten main tropical rain forest texts listed in Table 1. It was discovered that some form of tropical rain forest metalanguage comprised no less than 98 per cent of the texts, the remaining 2 per cent representing neutral facts about the Sites (or perhaps small errors in the lengthy coding procedures necessary for QSR NUD*IST 4). Overall, language use fell naturally into two main categories, which may be termed: (i) 'The Language of Needing' and (ii) 'The Language of Vulnerability'. There was a remarkable consistency between Sites in the percentage use of these two language categories, with 'The Language of Needing' predominating at a mean of 66 per cent.

Further analysis revealed that 'The Language of Needing' gives rise to the generation of three sets of modern hegemonic **Myths**. These are **Scientific Myths** (26%), **Economic Myths** (17%), and **Personal Myths** (23%), all with the specific aim of bolstering the contention that we '*need*' tropical rain forest for our ultimate survival. **Scientific** myth making develops two particular themes. First, tropical rain forest is constructed as a vital world ecological **Control System** (16% of total language use) maintaining the health of the whole planet (e.g. **TRC**[45]: 'They regulate earth's climate, are a deterrent against the greenhouse effect...' and **KQ**: '...vast areas of trees have been called the 'lungs of the earth'.'). Secondly in scientific terms, tropical rain forest is presented as an incomparable **Biodiversity** (10%) storehouse of genetic material, with enormous potential value for medicine, agriculture, and human welfare (e.g. **RA**: 'They are an untapped library of resources for medicine, food, human welfare and the global environment.').

---

[45] See Table 1 for the meaning of the acronyms given in **bold**. The sample quotations have been chosen to illustrate the type of language unit coded under each category.

(a) **(CI) Conservation International, Washington, DC**. URL: http://www.conservation.org/web/aboutci/rffacts.htm 'Tropical Rain Forest Facts' Page.　　　　　Accessed 10.00 on 6.8.1998.
(b) **(GP) Greenpeace International**. URL: http://www.greenpeace.org/~forests/ancient.html 'Ancient Forests' page (largely rain forests).　　Accessed 16.00 on 6.8.1998.
(c) **(KQ) Kids' Quest**. A Fundamentalist Christian Site, Arizona. URL: http://www.christiananswers.net/kids/kidshome.html The Science Page: 'Adventures in the Rain Forest...' 　　　　　　　　　　　　　　　Accessed 18.00 on 27.7.1998.
(d) **(RA) Rainforest Alliance**, New York, NY. URL: http://www.rainforest-alliance.org/ Rainforest Information Page　　　　　Accessed 16.00 on 22.7.1998.
(e) **(RAN) Rainforest Action Network**, San Francisco, CA. URL: http://www.ran.org/ran/ **(DR) Defenders of the Rainforest**. URL:http://www.hrc.wmin.ac.uk/campaigns/ef/rforest/defendhome.html 'Why rainforests are important?' Page.　　Accessed 15.30 on 23.7.1998.
(f) **(RIC) Rainforest Information Centre**, Lismore, NSW, Australia. URL: http://forests.org/ric/ 'Rainforests of the World Page'　　　　Accessed 16.45 on 23.7.1998.
(g) **(RPF) Rainforest Preservation Foundation**, Fort Worth, TX. URL: http://www.flash.net/~rpf/ 'Rainforest Information Page'.　　　　　Accessed 12.00 on 23.7.1998.
(h) **(RFPT) The Rain Forest Preservation Trust**, Charleston, SC. URL: http://www.rainforest-rpt.com/　　　　　Accessed July 1998.
i) **(RR) Rainforest Relief**, Brooklyn, NY (also Portland). URL: http://host.envirolink.org/rainrelief/ Some things you should know about the rainforest. Text is also used by (EC) Earth Culture, Greensboro, NC. URL:http://www.geocities.com/RainForest/3294 　　　　　　　　　　　　　　　Accessed 15.30 on 27.7.1998.
(j) **(TRC) Tropical Rainforest Coalition**, San Jose, CA. URL: http://www.rainforest.org/index.html 'Why care?' Page.　　　　　Accessed 16.00 on 22nd July 1998.

Table 1: The Web Sites employed in the Tropical Rain Forest
Language Study. 1998.

Economic myth making, by contrast, centres more directly on the economic value of, in particular, non-timber forest **Products** (9.2%), and ideas such as Extractive Reserves (e.g. **RIC**: 'All things have value in a natural forest no matter what their age or condition.'). The more **General** (7.8%) economic importance of tropical rain forest, for example in scientific and productive terms, is also elaborated (e.g. **RA**: 'After all, a healthy forest can provide a lot more than wood...' and **RA**: '... create a healthier, more equitable, and more productive planet.').

 Personal myth making is closely related to the assertion that our individual **Survival** (9%) in, say, Los Angeles, London and Berlin, depends specifically on the conservation of tropical rain forest (e.g. **RA**: 'Since our lives are so dependent on the forest's bounty...'). However, it also highlights our presumed moral and religious responsibilities for conserving tropical rain forest, sometimes relating these responsibilities to the probings of 'deep ecology' and New Age beliefs (e.g. **RIC**: 'Rainforests have been called the womb of life...' and **KQ**: 'We are reminded that trees are created to be pleasant...').

'The Language of Needing' is thus geared up to make us desperate to keep tropical rain forest at all costs. By contrast, the

 second major category of language use, 'The Language of Vulnerability' (32%), focuses on persuading us that the entity, tropical rain forest, is under severe threat from human actions. 'The Language of Vulnerability' divides naturally into two types, the first **Criminalising** (15% of total language use) human actions, the second underscoring, through the use of **Statistics** (17%), the shocking speed of tropical rain forest destruction and loss. **Criminalisation** is broken down into **Thoughtlessness** (5%) (e.g. **RPF**: 'We are driving species into extinction before we have identified them...') and positive **Greed** (10%) (e.g. **GP**: 'Most of these forests are being threatened by large industrial logging companies.'). The **Statistics** also come in two forms. The first are presented as absolute **'Facts'** (13%) (e.g. **GP**: '76 countries have already lost all of their large ancient forest areas' and **RFPT**: 'The World's rainforests are being destroyed at a rate of 150 acres per minute – 24 hours per day – 7 days per week.'). The second are what I term **Image Statistics** (4%), which aim to bring home to the reader, through analogy or metaphor, the very

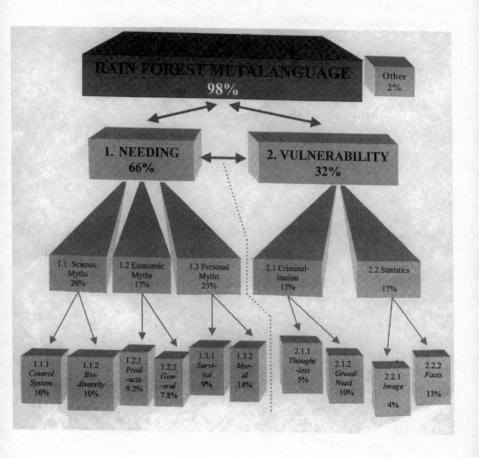

Figure 4. The results of the language analysis of 10 tropical rain forest documents on the World Wide Web, 1998. (See Table 1 for the details of all the sources used and the text for a full explanation.)

dramatic nature of the 'problem' (e.g. **CI**: '...an area of rain forest the size of New Hampshire and Vermont is cut annually' and **RIC**: '...about a football field a second...'). All this adds immediacy and passion to the myth-making process and demands a commensurate response.

Debunking the Myth, or Fighting the Hydra

Knowledge of ecology and forestry is poor among the public and understanding of ecosystem properties is almost absent while myths [my emphasis] abound especially with respect to tropical rain forests and their peoples. There is a certain unwillingness to bridge the knowledge gap and abandon inherited or newly developed myths if they serve self-interests. [46]

Professor E. F. Bruenig
(*Emeritus* Professor of Forestry,
Hamburg University).
Paper presented at Oxford University, 15th May 1998.

The 'Green' hegemonic myth of the 'tropical rain forest' is thus created. Essentially it is a European linguistic construction which has become an integral part of the Northern mindset and one which has little to do with any ecological reality or object in the tropical world and which deliberately excludes other forms and sources of myth making. [47]

The recent powerful imposition of this Northern mindset on to the less-developed countries (LDCs) of the tropics is probably both immoral and dangerous for the proper management of tropical environments. The whole process of subconscious and

---

[46] One particularly worrying aspect of the promulgation of the tropical rain forest myth, as well as certain parallel myths, such as that behind the idea of 'global warming', is the deliberate role played by many scientists in sustaining it. Often this is for their own political agenda, or simply because they believe that the 'end' they perceive to be 'good' justifies the means. The stance is frequently maintained *despite the fact that they do not personally accept the 'science' behind the myth*; they argue, however, that the 'collateral environmental' benefits outweigh the scientific uncertainty. See: Philip Stott, 'Biogeography and ecology in crisis: the urgent need for a new metalanguage.' *Journal of Biogeography* **25**(1) pp. 1–2 (1998).

[47] See for example: J. Wiens, 'On understanding a non-equilibrium world: myth and reality in community patterns and processes.' In: D. R. Strong, D. Simberloff, L.G. Abele & AB. Thistle (eds.), *Ecological communities: conceptual issues and the evidence*. Princeton. NJ: Princeton University Press, 439–457 (1984); D.B. Botkin, *Discordant harmonies. A new ecology for the Twenty-first Century*. New York & Oxford: Oxford University Press (1990); Sian Sullivan, 'Towards a non-equilibrium ecology: perspectives from an arid land. *Journal of Biogeography* **23**(1), pp. 1–5 (1996); Chapters 12 & 13 in Peter D. Moore, Bill Chaloner & Philip Stott, *Global Environmental Change*. Oxford: Blackwell Science (1996; rev. edn due out in 1999); P. Stott, 'Dynamic tropical forestry in an unstable world.' *Commonwealth Forestry Review* **76**(3), pp. 207–209 (1997).

conscious transfer should be regarded as a classic case of neo-colonialism by language, myth, and academic paradigm, and it represents a clear example of world political ecology in action. The North has controlled both the content and the meaning of the entity that it has created, and it has then attempted to impose this entity, with its mythical content, on the rest of the world through education, political activism, and at international fora. In essence, the myth is about maintaining intellectual power and hegemony, or, to recall the start of this essay, Humpty Dumpty's mastery over words and their meaning. This is why it is absolutely necessary to reveal, and to debunk, the fabric of the myth before it causes further damage, at the same time puncturing the bubble of false morality that so often envelops it.

The late-20th Century form of the myth

It must be recognised at once, however, that the late-20th Century form of the hegemonic myth is not an easy one to slay. In much of the media, it is simply taken as axiomatic that tropical rain forest is a 'good thing' and that untrammelled human greed and voraciousness unquestionably threaten the forest resource. Corrupt forest politics, illegal logging, and forest conflagrations all make splendid headlines. Tropical rain forest also competes with the 'evergreen' dinosaurs for a top place in Primary School art and science, while the tropical rain forest forms a natural moral focus, along with giant pandas and whales, for many idealistic young people in the North.

Additionally, the myth, through time, has grown into a mighty Hydra, with many different heads, each deriving its strength from one of the periods of myth making we have identified above. Cut off one of the mythic heads, and two more tend to appear, often more romantic and more dramatic than the last, the different mouths crying out the old myths in ever-newer forms, but especially:–

a) the European orientalist myths about the tropical world, dating from the 16th Century onwards;
b) the linguistic myth of the 'tropical rain forest', created at the very end of the 19th Century and solidified by Paul Richards in 1952;

c) the 'organis' iic' myths of the late-19th/early 20th Centuries, with their emphasis on equilibrium, balance, harmony, the optimum, and the 'ancient', undisturbed character of the tropical rain forest 'ecosystem';

d) the myth of the intrinsic vulnerability of the tropical rain forest Eden to human sin and greed, a myth which developed especially strongly from the 1930s onwards; and, finally,

e) the late-20th Century hegemonic scientific, economic, and personal myths which have been created to underpin the innate value and vulnerability of tropical rain forest in a modern world of uncontrolled economic globalisation.

To the above, we should probably add the mythical fears which are bound to attend the end of the Millennium. It is therefore hardly surprising that 86 per cent of the German people state that the loss of tropical rain forest is their chief worry, even though they will never visit the tropics and, to quote Professor Breunig, have a very poor 'knowledge of ecology and forestry'.

Slaying the Hydra

My final task, therefore, although I am no Hercules, must be to slay this mythical Hydra once and for all, hacking away in turn at each myth-spewing head.

First, science no longer views the world 'organismically'. In the 1920s, this essentially late-19th Century viewpoint was already under critical attack, even as Clements and Tansley were formulating their successional theories and their organismic concepts of the 'climax' and the 'optimum'.[48] By the 1960s and the1970s, the approach was virtually moribund, with writers such as Hugh Miller Raup, the Director of the famous Harvard Forest in Massachusetts (1946–1967), being able to write as early as 1957:

---

[48] See for example: H. A. Gleason, 'The individualistic concept of the plant association.' *Bulletin of the Torrey Botanical Club* **53**, pp. 7–26 (1926).

I see the plant community as a relatively loose aggregation of species, visible in the landscape, but not precisely definable in space or time.[49]

Furthermore, it was also becoming abundantly clear from palynology[50], and from other microfossil studies, that 'forests' do not persist or move in any sense as entities in response to environmental change. Rather, each individual species, and sometimes each individual, responds separately to change according to its own ecological parameters or ecological envelope.[51] There has therefore been a marked move away from the older *synecological* views of Schimper to a more *autecological* interpretation, one that stresses the inherent *individuality* of each species.[52] We are thus no longer concerned with the grouping of organisms into synthetic language units. What we perceive in the landscape as 'vegetation' is, in reality, only the particular mix of individuals at a given place at a given point in time. Any language construct, like 'tropical rain forest', can *never* relate to a clearly definable object, and, as asserted in the very first paragraph of this essay, 'tropical rain forest' simply does not exist as an object.

More importantly, however, the demise of the organismic viewpoint empowers us to lop off a great many more mythical heads from the Hydra. Obviously, the first to go must be the associated concepts of the 'climax' and the 'optimum'. As there are no permanent entities, there is nothing that can be recognized as an adult organism, nicely adjusted to a prevailing climate. Moreover, we now know that climate changes all the time,

---

[49] See: 'Obituary' in the *Annual Report of the Harvard Forest 1995–96*. Petersham, Mass.: Harvard Forest (1996). Hugh Miller Raup died in 1995.

[50] The study of pollen, in particular fossil pollen, which, because of their abundance in fossil peat and lake sediments, their inherent toughness, and the distinctive sculpturing of their outer coats, are ideal for reconstructing broad environmental changes in the past. See: P. D. Moore, J. A. Webb, & M.E. Collinson, *Pollen analysis*. Oxford: Blackwell Science, 2nd edn. (1991).

[51] This, for example, is especially clear in the brilliant synthesis by Professor H.J.K. Birks on the patterning of tree species in the British Isles during the post-glacial period (the Holocene) of the last 10,000 years. See: H.J.K. Birks, Holocene isochrone maps and patterns of tree-spreading in the British Isles. *Journal of Biogeography* **16** (6). 503–540 (1989).

[52] *Cf.* footnote 12.

gradually, catastrophically, and unpredictably, and that it changes in the tropics just as effectively as in the rest of the world.

Areas such as Amazonia and South East Asia, which are thought to have housed ancient tropical rain forest, up to 60 million years in age, were actually dominated, only 18,000 years ago, by plants and animals which recall the savanna grasslands of present-day East Africa. The Ice Ages of Eurasia and North America were accompanied in the tropics by periods of both colder and drier conditions, along with lower sea levels.[53] Some 16,000 years ago, the Malay Archipelago, today seen as the very bastion of the finest 'ancient' tropical rain forest, housed a 'savanna corridor', which ran from mainland South East Asia, with deeper sea gaps, to Papua New Guinea and Northern Australia (Figure 5).[54] Any 'tropical rain forest' that might have existed at the time would have been lost beneath the waters that ultimately formed the South China Sea when world sea levels rose eustatically with the melting of the great ice sheets. Some 12,000 years ago, Rondonia, in Brazil, was also probably savanna grassland. There is, therefore, simply *no* such entity as 'the ancient tropical rain forest', the millions-of-years-old Eden, untarnished by change and the human presence! The forested lands of the tropics are young, dynamic, and new, not old and stable. The species mix is constantly fluctuating between gaps, building phases, and maturer blocks of trees.[55]

The theoretical implications of these facts are very profound. As Hugh Miller Raup went on to argue: 'The ideas of community structure and the expression of dominance, that of biological succession, and finally, that of climax, are largely based on the assumption of long-term stability in the physical habitat. *Remove this assumption and the entire theoretical structure becomes a shambles*' (my italics). In other words, the

[53] See: Martin Kellman & Rosanne Tackaberry, *Tropical environments*. London & New York: Routledge (1997), especially Chapter 2.

[54] See for example: T.C. Whitmore (ed.), *The biogeographical evolution of the Malay Archipelago*. Oxford: Clarendon Press (1987).

[55] See: T.C. Whitmore. *An introduction to tropical rain forests*. Oxford: Clarendon Press (1990).

whole scientific basis for the 'tropical rain forest' hegemonic myth falls apart.

With the move to autecology, and the final recognition that climate changes all the time, there has inevitably been a concomitant shift away from the ideas of equilibrium, balance, harmony, and stability. Increasingly, research in every subject,

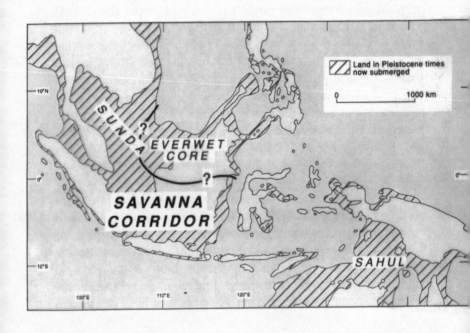

Figure 5. The ecology of South East Asia some 18,000 years ago. Note the presence of a 'savanna corridor'. (Adapted from: T. C. Whitmore (Ed.) (1987). *The biogeographical evolution of the Malay Archipelago*. Oxford: Clarendon Press).

ranging from anthropology to zoology, is showing us that we essentially live in a non-equilibrium world, in which the biological mix is constantly readjusted at all scales, all the time, by the forces of environmental change. Change must inevitably be taken as the norm, rather than stability of any kind.

For some ecologists, this has led to the recognition of what are termed 'stable limit cycles', with systems seen as alternating between two or more equilibria, but within set domains, or 'multiple equilibrium states', in which the systems stagger from one equilibrium to another. In many ways, these might be regarded as virtual contradictions in terms.[56] For other ecologists, including the present author, the revolution required is much more radical and demands the complete shedding, once and for all, of the equilibrium concept, and the acknowledgement that we need to develop a totally new metalanguage, much more in tune with the reality of constant environmental change.

Old key signifiers, such as 'balance', 'harmony', 'stability', as well as their associated modern totemic concepts like 'sustainability', which are ultimately derived from these signifiers, must now give way to a vibrant new language of 'change', 'instability', 'dynamism', 'surprise', 'risk', 'adaptability', 'opportunism', 'flexibility', 'movement', 'migration', 'resistance', 'resilience', 'uncertainty' and 'unpredictability'. Concepts like 'sustainable' and 'inviolate ancient forests', are inherently dangerous; what we should be looking for are new political, economic, and social programmes of 'flexible' development that can constantly adjust to change, as and when it happens. And the entities we decide to call 'forests' will come and go, as they always have. We no more *need* the 'tropical rain forest' than we did the 'mixed deciduous forest' that once grew over the very place where I have word-processed this essay. All is change, from the individual plant and animal, to the individual species, and thence to the whole biological mix that covers the Earth in an ever-varying kaleidoscopic pattern.

---

[56] J. Wiens, 'On understanding a non-equilibrium world: myth and reality in community patterns and processes.' In: D. R. Strong, D. Simberloff, L.G. Abele & AB. Thistle (eds.). *Ecological communities: conceptual issues and the evidence.* Princeton, NJ: Princeton University Press, 439–457 (1984).

We can thus conclude that 'tropical rain forest' does not exist and that it has never existed. Only a brief moment ago in geological time, there were hardly any trees at all in the areas of the world currently thought by so many people to have housed, for millions of years, the most complex ecosystem ever known, which they have constructed as 'tropical rain forest'. Moreover, there is no such thing as a stable climate to which an organismic entity can become adapted, because constant, gradual, catastrophic and unpredictable climate change is the norm. The world functions largely in non-equilibrium, with its biological components being endlessly remixed in response to change, so that 'forests' ebb and flow, with the world surviving unharmed. This is not a fragile Earth; it is an intrinsically restless Earth, flexible but ever tough.

It follows from all this that we must further slice away from the Hydra, and with particular vigour, the modern 'scientific' myths about the 'tropical rain forest' which were clearly revealed in the 1998 Language Survey reported earlier and which have been added on to the historic myths to give them more credence in the late-20th Century. Tropical rain forest has never been 'the dominant form of vegetation in the tropics for literally millions of years'. Likewise, it is not the most complex and biodiverse ecosystem on earth, the very concepts of 'ecosystem' and 'biodiversity' themselves being human constructs. And even if these did exist as such, tropical rain forest would have to compete for the trophy with many other entities, such as coral reefs, the deep oceans[57], the South African *fynbos*[58], not to mention the savannas.

Particularly risible, however, are the myths relating to the tropical rain forest as an ecological control system for the world. The most crass, without doubt, is the image of tropical rain forest as 'the lungs of the world'. The very metaphor means precisely the opposite of what is intended, demonstrating the sheer anarchy

---

[57] It is entirely arguable that the proper management of the oceans should have a far greater priority. The overemphasis on false issues, like the tropical rain forest, has often detracted from this fact.

[58] From Afrikaans: literally means 'fine-leaved bush'. *Fynbos* is a word used to describe a highly distinctive biome of open-to-closed, dwarf shrubby, shrub-woodland, found in the southwestern and southern Cape Province of South Africa. The *fynbos* biome approximates to the Cape Floristic Kingdom, where plant diversity is probably higher than anywhere else in the world.

of the myth-making process. 'Lungs', of course, *take in oxygen and give out carbon dioxide*, which is not at all what is envisaged by the 'Green' discourse. The metaphor is meant to indicate that tropical rain forest gives out life-giving oxygen and takes in that dreadfully worrying 'greenhouse gas', carbon dioxide. Unfortunately for the discourse, the use of the metaphor tends to backfire badly, in that it can often prove quite apposite, with many areas in the tropics dominated by trees possessing heavy decomposition systems, which really do ensure a strong up-take of oxygen!

Equally nonsensical, however, are the direct attempts to blame the cutting and burning of tropical rain forest for the perceived problems of 'global warming'. Without 200 years of industrial development in the North, the subject of global warming would never even have raised its ugly head. Any attempt to transfer blame to the South is morally outrageous, especially when we remember that, despite human deforestation, there are probably still more trees in the tropics than there were only 16,000 years ago at the end of the last Ice Age. Moreover, recent research in West Africa has raised serious doubts about some of the international statistics with regard to deforestation, undermining considerably many of the absolute statistics and image myths so eagerly employed to 'dramatise' the overall loss of trees and 'forest'.[59]

It is also worth remembering that tropical forests and savannas have always burned, on cycles varying from one to two years in the savannas, to longer-term cycles in the forests. The more stochastic fire events are often associated with catastrophic weather patterns, like the El Niño Southern Oscillation (ENSO)[60], a mighty force for change. Important El Niño fires have been recorded in Borneo, for example, in 1878–84, 1914–15, 1958,

---

[59] See the important ground-breaking work of James Fairhead & Melissa Leach, *Misreading the African landscape. Society and ecology in a forest-savanna mosaic*. Cambridge: Cambridge University Press (1996).

[60] Philip Stott, 'The forest as phoenix: towards a biogeography of fire in mainland South East Asia.' *The Geographical Journal* **154** (3), pp. 227–350 (1988); for El Niño fire events, visit the 'Integrated Forest Fire Management Project (IFFM), Indonesia' Web Site at: http://smd.mega.net.id/iffm/.

1969–70, 1982–83, 1991, and, most recently, the heavily if much misreported fires of 1997–98.

'J'accuse!'

Where the views of landscape which are driving policy are demonstrably false, greater historical precision renders clearly apparent their relations of power and sometimes their brutal material effects.

James Fairhead & Melissa Leach,
Misreading the African landscape:
Society and ecology in a forest-savanna mosaic.
Cambridge: Cambridge University Press,
p.292 (1996).

In the light of these advances made in ecology during the last 50 or so years, it is unacceptable that the late-20th Century excrescence of the tropical rain forest historic and hegemonic myth has been allowed to hold sway over us, so disturbingly, for so long. The time has surely come to acknowledge our self-deceit, a deceit that is no longer tenable, whatever the causes of our inability to cope with the glare of exposure.[61]

It may well be true that, in the North, with our residual Christian, and especially Protestant, values, we have felt a deep guilt about the historical treatment of our own landscape and 'forests', which, in Europe and eastern North America, were largely cleared by the 17th and 18th Centuries.[62] We may also be seeking to find a new classical Golden Age, so that, with the Duke in *As you like it*, we can go once again to live 'in the Forest of Arden ... as they did in the golden world'.[63] We may even regard the tropical rain forest as a last pure Eden on Earth, the very 'optimum' of Clements and Tansley, an 'Eden of perfect rainfall

---

[61] E.g. D.B. Botkin. *Discordant harmonies. A new ecology for the Twenty-first Century.* New York & Oxford: Oxford University Press (1990) and Anna Bramwell, *The fading of the Greens.* New Haven & London: Yale University Press (1994).

[62] See for example: W. Cronon, *Changes in the Land. Indians, Colonists and the Ecology of New England.* Hill & Wang: New York (1983); G.G. Whitney, *From Coastal Wilderness to Fruited Plain: a History of Environmental Change in Temperate North America from 1500 to the Present.* Cambridge University Press: Cambridge (1994).

[63] William Shakespeare. in *As you like it* (Act 1. Scene 1).

and equability, against which all other habitats must be assessed.'[64] We may indeed be desperately seeking to hold on to this icon of 'ancient stability' in the face of rampant global capitalism and constant change, or feel ourselves to be at one with the life force of the trees and the Earth. And, whilst we may genuinely feel for the plight of forest peoples, we forget that the very act of finding and naming brings control and the inevitable 'human zoo'.

But none of these is any longer acceptable, either as excuses or as explanations. They represent a Northern agenda, our own guilt, our own anxieties, our own desires, our own self-indulgences, and we can no longer be permitted to foist them, wittingly or unwittingly, on the rest of the world, a world which needs to develop quickly and to grow rapidly in its own right and own manner. We have constantly and wilfully misread other peoples' landscapes; we have appropriated their history and so often proceeded to replace it with a false history of our own construction.[65]

The 'Great Green Anglo-Saxon Hegemonic Myth'[66] of the 'tropical rain forest' has thus been constructed and deconstructed. Yet, it still holds sway over much of the media, on television, on radio, and in the press. It must now be discredited and discarded as quickly as possible. As Dr Tomas Stockman declaims in Henrik Ibsen's masterpiece, *An Enemy of the People* (1882):

---

[64] P. Stott. 'Dynamic tropical forestry in an unstable world.' *Commonwealth Forestry Review* 76(3), (1997). p. 208. Column 2.

[65] See especially: James Fairhead & Melissa Leach, *Misreading the African landscape. Society and ecology in a forest-savanna mosaic*. Cambridge: Cambridge University Press (1996) and James Fairhead & Melissa Leach, *Reframing deforestation. Global analysis and local realities: studies in West Africa*. London & New York: Routledge (1998).

[66] Elsewhere I have referred to the myth as 'Little Green Lies'; see Peter D. Moore, Bill Chaloner & Philip Stott. *Global Environmental Change*. Oxford: Blackwell Science (1996; rev. edn due out in 1999), p. 211. One scientific colleague remarked that 'Big Green Whoppers' would be much nearer to the mark.

What sort of truths do the majority usually embrace? Truths that are so decrepit, they're on the way to being senile. And when a truth has lasted that long, gentlemen, it's well on the way to being a lie.[67]

Equally, a new metalanguage must urgently be found, one which takes change and instability as the norm, and one which mirrors far more realistically the ever-dynamic character of the Earth, not to mention the intrinsically dynamic ecology of the tropics and the tropical world. In accepting this, however, and in acknowledging that we can no longer support outdated theories of stability, equilibrium, and 'forests as inviolate entities', we must also be especially careful to give no succour *whatsoever* to the continued production of landscapes of fear and despair. We provide no mandate for illegal logging, poor silivicultural practices, bad development theory, the misuse of fire, and Mafia-like pioneer politics. In fact, our moral responsibilities are precisely the opposite and probably all the greater. We must strive even more to ensure that the systems replacing the trees are truly productive and flexible systems, fully adapted to an ever-changing, unstable, non-equilibrium world.

---

[67] Henrik Ibsen [1882], *An Enemy of the People*. A new version by Christopher Hampton. London & Boston: Faber and Faber, p. 92 (1997). First performed at the Royal National Theatre's Olivier Theatre on 12th September 1997, with Ian McKellen as Stockman.

Selected Further Readings and Resources

Atkinson, A (1991). *Principles of political ecology*. London: Belhaven.

Bennett, J. & W. Chaloupka (Eds.). *In the Nature of Things: language, politics, and the environment*. Minneapolis: University of Minnesota Press.

Botkin, D.B. (1990). *Discordant harmonies. A new ecology for the Twenty-first Century*. New York & Oxford: Oxford University Press.

Bowers, J. (1997). *Sustainability and environmental economics. An alternative text*. Harlow, Essex: Addison Wesley Longman.

Bramwell, A. (1994). *The fading of the Greens. The decline of environmental politics in the West*. New Haven & Yale: Yale University Press.

Bryant, R.L. (1992). 'Political ecology: an emerging research agenda in Third-world studies.' *Political Geography* 11, pp. 12–36.

Bryant, R. L. & S. Bailey (1997). *Third World political ecology*. London & New York: Routledge.

Bryant, R.L., J. Rigg & P. Stott (Eds.) (1993). 'The political ecology of southeast Asian forests: transdisciplinary discourses.' *Global Ecology and Biogeography Letters* 4 (4–6), pp. 101–296.

Cittadino, E. (1990). *Nature as the laboratory. Darwinian plant ecology in the German Empire, 1880–1900*. Cambridge: Cambridge University Press.

DeAngelis, D.L. & J.C. Waterhouse (1987). 'Equilibrium and nonequilibrium concepts in ecological models.' *Ecological Monographs* 57, 1–21.

Desai, U. (Ed.) (1998). *Ecological policy and politics in developing countries. Economic growth, democracy, and environment*. Albany: State University of New York Press.

Fairhead, J. & M. Leach (1996). *Misreading the African landscape. Society and ecology in a forest-savanna mosaic.* Cambridge: Cambridge University Press.

Fairhead, J. & M. Leach (1998). *Reframing deforestation. Global analysis and local realities: studies in West Africa.* London & New York: Routledge.

Grove, R. H., V. Damodaran & S. Sangwan (Eds.) (1998). *Nature and the Orient. The environmental history of South and Southeast Asia.* Delhi: Oxford University Press.

Integrated Forest Fire Management Project (IFFM), Indonesia, Web Site (1999): URL: http://smd.mega.net.id/iffm/

Jackson, J.B.C., A.F. Budd & A.G. Coates (Eds.) (1996). *Evolution and environment in Tropical America.* Chicago: University of Chicago Press.

Kalland, A. & G. Persoon (Eds.) (1998). *Environmental movements in Asia.* Richmond, Surrey: Curzon Press.

Kellman, M. & R. Tackaberry (1997). *Tropical environments.* London and New York: Routledge.

Leach, M., J. Fairhead & D. Millimouno (1997). *Second Nature: building forests in West Africa's savanna.* **Video**: Haywards Heath, West Sussex: Cyrus Productions.

Leach, M. & R. Mearns (Eds.) (1996). *The lie of the land: challenging received wisdom on the African environment.* London, Oxford & Portsmouth: The International African Institute, James Currey & Heinemann.

Moore, P. D., W. Chaloner & P. Stott (1996). *Global environmental change.* Oxford: Blackwell Science.

Pimm, S.L. (1991). *The balance of nature?* Chicago: University of Chicago Press.

Roberts, N. (1998). *The Holocene. An environmental history.* Oxford and Malden, Massachusetts: Blackwell.

Said, E. (1993). *Culture and imperialism.* London: Chatto & Windus.

Sarup, M. (1993). *An introductory guide to post-structuralism and postmodernism.* 2nd edn. Hemel Hempstead, Herts: Harvester Wheatsheaf.

Savage, G. (1984). *Western impressions of Nature and landscape in South-East Asia.* Singapore: Singapore University Press.

Society of American Foresters Web Site (1999): URL: http://www.safnet.org/index.html

Stott, P. (1997). 'Dynamic forestry in an unstable world.' *Commonwealth Forestry Review* **76** (3), 207–209.

Stott, P. (1998). 'Biogeography and ecology in crisis: the urgent need for a new metalanguage.' *Journal of Biogeography* **25**(1), 1–2.

Stott, P. (1999). *The Anti-Ecohype Web Site*:

URL: http://ourworld.compuserve.com/homepages/stott2/

UK Tropical Forest Forum Web Site (1999): URL: http://www.nri.org/TFF/homepage.htm

Whitmore, T.C. (1984). *Tropical rain forests of the Far East.* 2nd edn. Oxford: Clarendon Press.

Whitmore, T.C. (Ed.) (1987). *The biogeographical evolution of the Malay Archipelago.* Oxford: Clarendon Press.

Whitmore, T.C. (1990). *An introduction to tropical rain forests.* Oxford: Clarendon Press.

Zimmermann, F (1987). *The jungle and the aroma of meats. An ecological theme in Hindu medicine.* Berkeley: University of California Press.